SACRAMENTO PUBLIC LIBRARY

808

D1548853

3RARY

SACRAMENTO, CA 95814

3/2006

Exploring Ancient

GREECE

with Elaine Landau

Enslow Elementary

an imprint of

Enslow Publishers, Inc.

40 Industrial Road   PO Box 38
Box 398   Aldershot
Berkeley Heights, NJ 07922   Hants GU12 6BP
USA   UK

http://www.enslow.com

Enslow Elementary, an imprint of Enslow Publishers, Inc.

Enslow Elementary® is a registered trademark of Enslow Publishers, Inc.

Copyright © 2005 by Elaine Landau

All rights reserved.

No part of this book may be reproduced by any means
without the written permission of the publisher.

Library of Congress Cataloging-in-Publication Data:

Landau, Elaine.
    Exploring ancient Greece with Elaine Landau / Elaine Landau.
        p. cm. — (Exploring ancient civilizations with Elaine Landau)
    Includes bibliographical references and index.
    ISBN 0-7660-2342-7
    1. Greece—Civilization—To 146 B.C.—Juvenile literature. I. Title. II. Series.
    DF77.L326 2005
    938—dc22

2004028111

Printed in the United States of America

10 9 8 7 6 5 4 3 2 1

To Our Readers: We have done our best to make sure all Internet Addresses in this book were active and appropriate when we went to press. However, the author and the publisher have no control over and assume no liability for the material available on those Internet sites or on other Web sites they may link to. Any comments or suggestions can be sent by e-mail to comments@enslow.com or to the address on the back cover.

All illustrations of Elaine and Max are ©David Pavelonis unless otherwise noted.

Illustration Credits: Ancient Art & Architecture Collection Ltd © AAAC / Topham / The Image Works, p. 25 (top); © Topham / The Image Works, p. 8; © The British Museum / HIP / The Image Works , pp. 17, 36 (top), 37 (bottom), 38 (right); The British Museum / Topham / The Image Works, p. 18; © Photos.com, pp. i, 5, 7, 12, 30 (Athena and Zeus), 31(top), 35 (inset), 45; ©Enslow Publishers, Inc., pp. 4–5 (map), 11 (map), 30 (Drawings of Aphrodite, Atlas, Gaia, Hades, Persephone, Prometheus); © Corporation of London / HIP / The Image Works, p. 11 (inset); © Corel Corporation, pp. 9, 12, 13, 19, 23 (top), 28, 29 (top), 30 (Hermes and Poseidon), 31 (bottom), 33 (top), 35 (top), 39 (top), 40, 41 (top), 44, 46; © Associated Press, AP / Julie Jacobson, Staff, p. 39 (bottom); © Clipart.com, pp. 4, 10, 15, 20, 21 (top), 23 (bottom), 25 (bottom), 26, 30 (Demeter), 32, 34, 37 (top), 38 (left, top); ©ARPL / HIP / The Image Works, p. 16; © AAAC / Topham / The Image Works, p. 6; © 2004 Werner Forman / Topham / The Image Works, p. 38 (left, bottom); ©2004 Werner Forman / TopFoto / The Image Works, p. 22.

Front Cover Credits: © Corel Corporation: The Parthenon, main image; Vase de Vix, Musee de Chatillon-sur-Seine (bottom, right); Greek Vase painting depicting javelin throwing riders, Panathenaic amphora, 4th century B.C. ©AAAC / Topham / The Image Works (top, right).

Back Cover Credits: © Corel Corporation: Zeus, Museum of Olympia, Greece

Contents

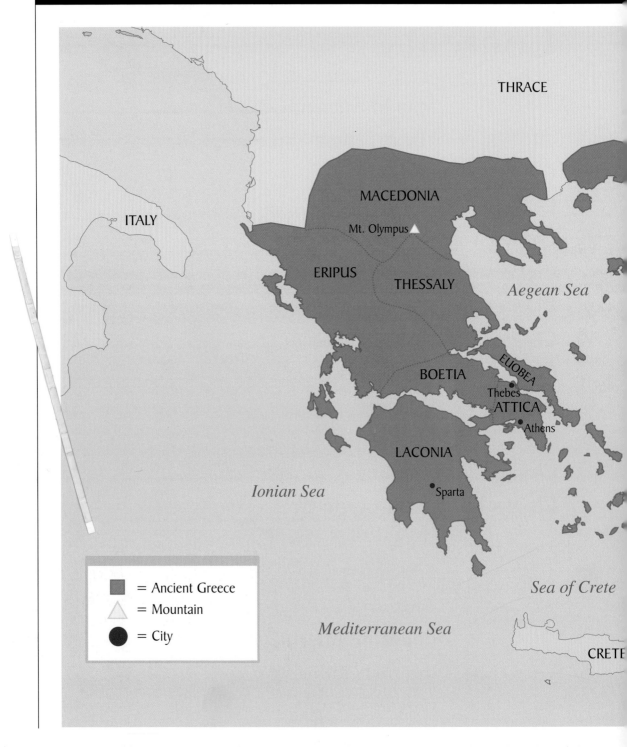

THRACE

MACEDONIA

Mt. Olympus △

ITALY

ERIPUS

THESSALY

Aegean Sea

EUOBEA

BOETIA

Thebes

ATTICA

Athens

LACONIA

Ionian Sea

Sparta

■ = Ancient Greece

△ = Mountain

● = City

Sea of Crete

Mediterranean Sea

CRETE

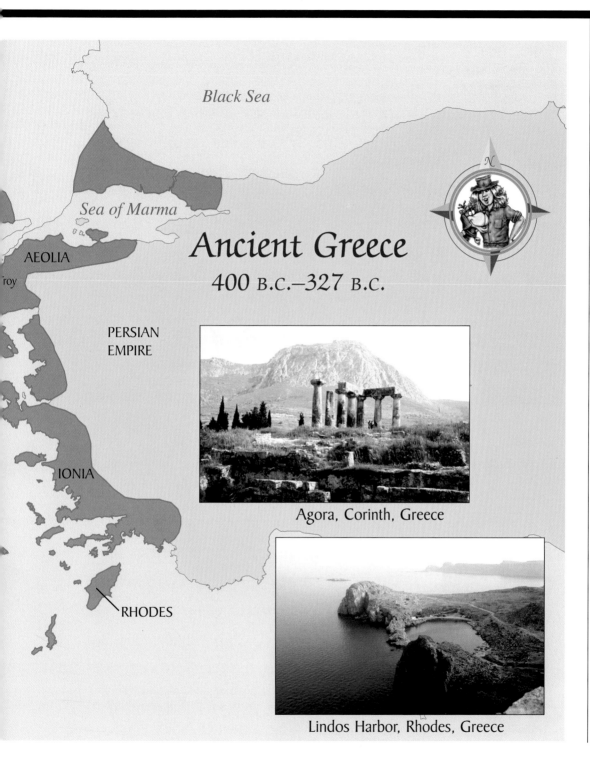

Black Sea

Sea of Marma

AEOLIA

Troy

PERSIAN
EMPIRE

IONIA

RHODES

Ancient Greece
400 B.C.–327 B.C.

Agora, Corinth, Greece

Lindos Harbor, Rhodes, Greece

Dear Fellow Explorer,

What if you could use a time machine to travel back in time? If you could go anywhere in the world, where would you stop? Perhaps you would like to visit an ancient civilization.

If so, I have a special place in mind. It is a small country in southeast Europe. But it was once a major center of the ancient world. The people there made amazing gains in different areas. They were gifted sculptors and architects. They built magnificent temples and statues.

They were far ahead of other countries. These people were also outstanding mathematicians and astronomers. They reached new heights in both theater and sports. The Olympics started there and were held there until A.D. 393.

The people of this ancient land were among the greatest thinkers and writers of all time. They wrote numerous outstanding plays, books, and poems. Many of these are still studied in schools. This highly advanced

This ancient Greek vase from the fourth century B.C. shows riders on horses throwing javelins at targets. The standing javelin throw was an event at the ancient Olympics.

Visitors to Athens are greeted with ancient buildings on the city's skyline.

civilization even gave the United States its form of government—democracy. Citizens took part in government, just like Americans do today.

By now you may have guessed the place I am describing. It is ancient Greece. Ancient Greece reached the height of its glory during the 400s and 300s B.C. This was a time of discovery and wonder. It was known as the Golden Age.

I am Elaine Landau, and this is my dog Max. We are about to take a trip back in time to ancient Greece. The trip was Max's idea. He has always wanted to go to the Olympics. Come along with us. There is a lot to see. Don't worry. We won't be late! With time travel, you can reach your destination right away. Just turn the page!

DON'T WORRY, MAX. YOU WON'T BE SPENDING MUCH TIME ON THE BEACH. THERE ARE TOO MANY INTERESTING THINGS TO SEE IN ANCIENT GREECE.

I SHOULD HAVE BROUGHT MY SWIMSUIT AND SUNGLASSES.

History

Much of Greece is a mountainous peninsula. It was surrounded by the Mediterranean Sea. The nearby islands were also part of ancient Greece. So was a portion of the land we now know as the country of Turkey.

Ancient Greece's civilization started in about 2000 B.C. At first, small farming villages formed on the mainland. By the 1600s B.C., many of these villages had grown into towns. A king ruled each town. Many had fortresses and waged war on one another.

Mycenae (my-SEE-nee) was among the largest, richest, and strongest towns. Its people built beautiful palaces. They also made advances in the arts. They traded with civilizations as far off as Egypt.

The Mycenaeans (my-se-NEE-uhns) were also conquerors. They invaded the nearby island of Crete. They took over towns on the mainland as well. That is why this time in Greece's history is known as the Mycenaean period.

A mask of beaten gold was found placed over the face of a dead Mycenaean king.

The Treasury of Atreus was built during the Mycenaean period. Kings were usually buried in these chambers. Because of the many beautiful objects buried with them, these graves were known as "Treasuries."

However, the Mycenaeans' glory did not last. By about 1200 B.C., Mycenae was overrun by foreign invaders. Its sparkling culture soon crumbled. For the next four hundred years, Greece went through a time known as the Dark Age.

During the Dark Age, people lived in small towns. These towns had little to do with one another. Interest in the arts faded.

Yet, memories of the Mycenaean period were kept alive. This was done through long epic poems. Such poems were filled with adventure, daring, and heroic deeds. These poems were sung by wandering bards or poets.

By about 800 B.C., the Dark Age was over. The small towns had grown into city-states.

Each city-state was proud and independent. The different city-states had their own governments. They also had their own gods to protect them.

Mountains or the sea separated most of the city-states. Yet people still kept in touch with one another. They shared the same language and customs.

The new city-states achieved greatness. Between 800 and 500 B.C., many important and exciting advances were

The ancient Greek city-states often fought against invaders. Here, Spartans battle the Persians at Salamis. More than eight hundred Persian ships were rammed and shattered by the Greeks.

made in art, science, theater, and government.

The ancient Greeks also established colonies in many regions. These included the areas we know today as Sicily and Italy. They had colonies along the Black Sea and the Aegean Sea.

At times, the ancient Greek city-states banded together to fight off foreign invaders. In 490 B.C., they defeated the Persian army at the Battle of Marathon. Then in 480 B.C., they again defeated invading Persian forces in the Battle of Salamis.

But other nations hoped to conquer the Greek city-states as well. This was true of Macedonia—a country to the north of Greece. In 338 B.C., Macedonia's King Philip II defeated the Greeks at the Battle of Chaeronea. Philip II's son, Alexander, had helped him win this victory.

Philip II made an interesting bargain with the Greeks. He promised to withdraw his troops. He would also allow the Greek city-states to govern themselves. But in return, the city-states had to join together in a league. Being part of the league meant that they had to follow Philip II into battle. King Philip II never lived to see this happen.

He was killed before the league was put together. However, Alexander, his son, took over.

In 334 B.C., Alexander set about conquering Persia with a combined Greek and Macedonian army. Soon, he became known as Alexander the Great. In the years that followed, Alexander took over much of the Persian Empire. As a result, Greek culture was spread to different parts of the world.

In the 140s B.C., Rome took over both Macedonia and Greece. As the Romans conquered other lands, they spread Greek culture. The Greek influence in art, politics, and science is still felt today.

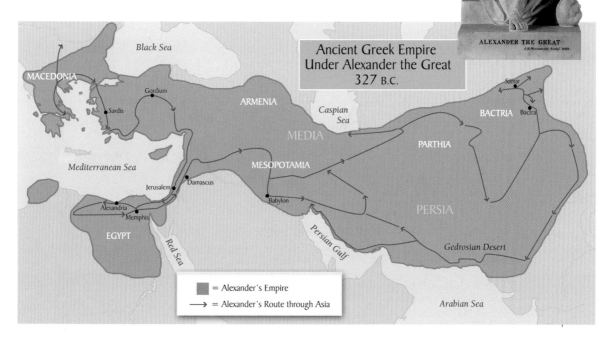

ALEXANDER THE GREAT
J.G.Wentworth Sculp! 1868.

Ancient Greek Empire
Under Alexander the Great
327 B.C.

Black Sea

MACEDONIA

Gordium

Sardis

ARMENIA

Caspian
Sea

MEDIA

BACTRIA   Bactra

Samar

PARTHIA

Mediterranean Sea

MESOPOTAMIA

Jerusalem   Damascus

Babylon

Alexandria
Memphis

EGYPT

Red Sea

Persian Gulf

PERSIA

Gedrosian Desert

Arabian Sea

= Alexander's Empire
⟶ = Alexander's Route through Asia

Athens and Sparta

*T*he city-states of ancient Greece were not all alike. Each developed in its own way. Two of the best-known city-states were Athens and Sparta. They were fierce rivals. Each believed that its way of life was the best. Both also wanted to be the greater power. Spartans were known to be especially jealous of Athenians.

Athens was home to some of Greece's most respected thinkers, writers, and artists. It was also a center for great architecture and sculpture. The Athenians built an impressive outdoor theater. There was a luxurious music hall and beautiful bathhouses.

The Acropolis was the center of life for the Athenians.

The Parthenon was built to honor the goddess Athena.

According to myth, Athena sprang, fully formed, from the head of her father, Zeus. Statues of Athena sometimes show her holding Zeus's head as this one does.

The Acropolis (uh-KROP-uh-lihs) is a steep hill in Athens' center. The Athenians constructed some magnificent temples and statues there. The Parthenon (PAHR-thuh-nahn) is the most famous of these. It is a large rectangular white marble temple. The Parthenon was built to honor the

goddess Athena. Completed in 432 B.C., it took fifteen years to build. Inside the Parthenon was a large gold and ivory statue of the goddess Athena.

The city-state of Sparta was not like Athens. Spartans did not fill their lives with beauty and comfort. Sparta was a military state. There, all the men trained to be soldiers. The army and loyalty to the state were highly valued.

At seven years of age, Spartan boys left their mothers. They were sent to military school by the state. They trained to be tough as well as physically fit. They also learned discipline. Spartan boys were expected to handle hardships and pain. Sometimes they had to walk long distances without shoes. They also bathed in freezing river waters.

Spartans believed in a simple life. They disliked any form of weakness. In Sparta, strength, obedience, and great courage were what counted.

The Spartans feared that Athens was becoming too strong. So in 431 B.C., Sparta and its allies attacked Athens. This marked the start of the Peloponnesian (peh-luh-puh-NEE-zhehn) War. This war lasted about twenty-seven years. The fighting only stopped during a seven-year truce.

During the war, both city-states enjoyed some victories. Sparta had the better army. However, Athens was protected by a thick wall. Even Sparta's well-trained soldiers could not get past it.

Athens also had a superior fleet. So Athenians behind the wall could still get food and other supplies. It was brought to them by ship.

This plan protected Athens for a time. But then Athens' navy suffered a heavy defeat. Without food and water, the Athenians were forced to open their gates. This led to Sparta winning the war. Nevertheless, Athens later regained its independence.

The Athenians were defeated at the Battle of Syracuse, the greatest single disaster in Athens' history.

Society

Males enjoyed most of the rights and freedoms in ancient Greece. Men also made the laws and did the governing. The man was the head of the household as well. Husbands were supposed to support, protect, and care for their wives.

Women were expected to care for the home and children. They prepared the meals. They also spent a lot of time spinning and weaving cloth.

On this shallow bowl, teachers and students are seen going through their lessons. A pupil can be seen playing the aulos, a flute with a double reed.

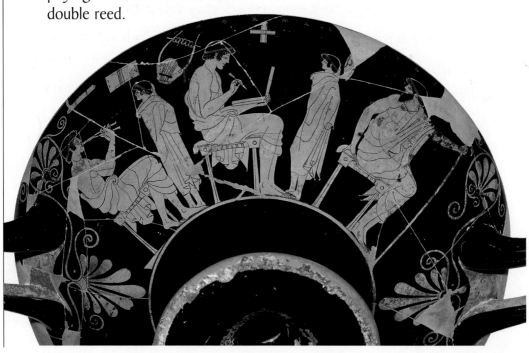

Athenian women had very little freedom. They did not go to parties with friends. Women rarely left their homes. However, they did go to weddings, funerals, and some festivals honoring the gods.

In Athens, young boys went to school. Some rich

I SERIOUSLY DOUBT IT, MAX.

WOULD A FABULOUS DOG LIKE ME HAVE HAD A PRIVATE TRAINER?

families hired private tutors for their male children. The boys studied science, math, music, and physical education. They trained to be good citizens. Girls were not educated the same way. Their mothers taught them how to care for a home. Girls from wealthy families learned how to read and write as well.

Poorer children in Athens did not attend school. The boys learned a trade. They might become stonemasons, metalsmiths, or

Women in ancient Greece made the family's clothes. This painting from 490 B.C. shows a woman spinning wool into thread.

carpenters. Mothers taught their daughters to be homemakers.

Things were different in Sparta. There, boys lived in military schools from the ages of seven to twenty. At twenty they became soldiers. They also married. Yet the soldiers stayed at the army barracks for ten more years. At thirty they went home to live with their wives and children. That did not mean their military service was over. They remained soldiers until old age.

Spartan women were fairly well treated. They were more highly thought of than in

This Spartan girl is running a race. She looks back over her shoulder to see how far she is in the lead. Spartan girls were not trained to fight in wars, but, like the boys, they were trained in running and for life in the outdoors.

other city-states. Sparta required that women be educated and physically fit.

Women in Sparta ran their households while their husbands lived in the army barracks. The same was true when the men were off fighting. Spartan women made important decisions each day.

Slaves were used throughout ancient Greece. These were often people captured in wars. Slaves did much of the hard physical work. They worked in homes, fields, and shops. Slaves were the property of their owners. They had few rights.

A Spartan charioteer rides into battle.

4 Government

ncient Greece is known as the birthplace of democracy. Democracy means "rule by the people." In a democracy, the people hold the most power. They rule themselves, or through people that they elect into the government.

Around 500 B.C., the ancient Greeks decided that they wanted a better form of government. They overthrew their unfair leaders. Many city-states began to build themselves into democracies.

The city-state of Athens was the best example of a working democracy in ancient Greece. There, all male citizens could have a say in government. They had the right to vote. They could serve on juries. Male citizens were also able to speak their minds freely.

Pericles (PEHR-uh-KLEEZ) was one of Athens' greatest statesmen. He headed Athens' government for

Male citizens were able to speak their minds freely in government councils.

Pericles did much to improve Greek society.

over thirty years. Pericles was from a noble family. Yet he cared about the common people. In 457 B.C., he helped see to it that male commoners could hold any government office. It was an important step in building a true democracy.

Nevertheless, the system was not perfect. Some rich Athenians had more advantages than other people. At times, government officials also tried to unfairly sway voters. Women, slaves, and foreigners in Athens were not allowed to vote. They could not help decide who should win a court case either.

Sparta had a different form of government. That city-state was governed by a group of men. These included two kings, some elders, and an assembly. The free men of Sparta elected the assembly. Five ephors were also part of this group. Ephors were judges who had some power over the kings.

MAX, WOULD YOU HAVE RATHER LIVED IN ATHENS OR SPARTA?

I WOULD DEFINITELY PICK ATHENS. EVEN THOUGH THEIR DEMOCRACY WAS NOT PERFECT, THEY WERE HEADED IN THE RIGHT DIRECTION.

5 World of Work

Many ancient Greeks farmed the land. Often they had small family farms. They usually worked these alone or with one or two slaves. At busy times, the wives and children helped.

Some rich landowners had larger farms. They had many slaves to do the heavy farmwork. They also hired poor men who had no land of their own.

Ancient Greek farmers could not grow a wide range of crops. The soil was too poor. They mainly grew barley, olives, grapes, and some wheat. They also grew some fruits and vegetables.

THESE GRAPES ARE DELICIOUS. I WOULD RATHER EAT THAN FARM ANY DAY.

Not everyone farmed. There were many fishermen in areas near the water. There were also talented craftsmen in ancient Greece. They made pottery, weapons and armor, clothing, tools, and jewelry.

An amulet from 1 B.C. shows a Greek farmer harvesting his crops.

Sculptors created fine works of art, like this bust of the Greek god Zeus.

Most had workshops in town. These were centered around the open marketplace known as the agora.

The ancient Greeks could not grow or make everything they needed. So some men became merchant traders. They traded with the Greek colonies. They also sailed to other countries to buy and sell things.

Other people in ancient Greece were doctors, architects, poets, artists, and sculptors.

Forgers of armor and weapons

Musicians

Artists

Art and Science

*T*he Golden Age was an important period in ancient Greece. Many advances made in math and science lasted through the ages.

The ancient Greek mathematician Euclid developed the principles of geometry. Geometry is a form of math that deals with lines and angles. Ancient Greek mathematicians were even able to find the earth's circumference. The ancient Greece astronomer Aristarchus (ar-ih-STAHR-kuhs) of Samos correctly argued that Earth revolved around the sun. Other ancient

peoples believed that the sun and other planets revolved around Earth. The ancient Greek scientist Democritus (dih-MAH-kruh-tuhs) had the idea that everything was made up of tiny particles. Today we call these atoms.

The ancient Greeks also developed new methods of questioning and thinking about things. This was called

In his search to find the truth and in his efforts to teach young Athenians to reason, Socrates disregarded his personal safety. He was condemned to death by the Athenians for standing up for what he believed.

Plato wrote down his beliefs in a book called the *Republic*. In his most famous work, he tells about the ideal state and the kind of education that should be given to young men to make them good citizens.

philosophy. The word philosophy means "love of wisdom." Greek philosophers pondered (thought about) serious questions.

Some of the greatest philosophers of ancient times were Greeks. The philosopher Socrates (SAH-kruh-teez) and his student Plato were among them. Aristotle (AR-ih-stat-uhl) was another great ancient Greek philosopher. He was Alexander the Great's teacher when the ruler was a boy.

Ancient Greek sculptors created magnificent pieces. Their statues were lifelike. Many seemed to show emotions. The pottery made in ancient Greece was superior as well. Artists painted lively designs on their vases and bowls. These frequently featured animals, people, and sea creatures.

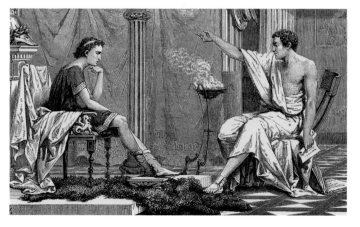

Aristotle (right) teaches a young Alexander the Great. For two thousand years after Aristotle's death, his books on astronomy, mathematics, poetry, physics, logic, and rhetoric (speaking and writing) were studied by students, as the highest authority in all matters of science and philosophy.

Ancient Greek architects built splendid temples and government buildings. Often these had columns, balconies, and covered outdoor walkways. Such structures were quite spacious and beautiful.

Literature (written stories) blossomed during the Golden Age. Earlier, in the 800s and 700s B.C., epic poems had been popular. Two of the most famous of these are *The Iliad* (IH-lee-uhd) and *The Odyssey* (oh-DIH-see-uhs). They were written by the Greek poet Homer.

The Iliad is about the last year of the Trojan War. According to legend, this was a ten-year war between Greece and the city of Troy. Troy was an ancient city in the country we now know as Turkey. In the poem, the Trojan War is fought over a beautiful woman named Helen.

The Odyssey is an adventure story. Its main character is Ithaca's King Odysseus (oh-DIH-see-uhs). *The Odyssey* is the tale of Odysseus' difficult sea voyage home from the Trojan War.

The great wooden horse loomed at the gates of Troy after the Greek besiegers had apparently withdrawn. The Trojans, curious, brought it into their city. At night, the Greeks emerged from the wooden horse and captured the city. Homer tells this story in the *Iliad*.

Little is known about Homer. However, he was supposed to have been blind. Some historians think that Homer may not have existed. They believe that several different poets created *The Iliad* and *The Odyssey*. Others think that Homer asked other poets to write them down for him when he was very old. By then, the Greeks had developed a form of writing.

During the Golden Age, lyric poetry became popular. Lyric poems were shorter than epic poems. This poetry was different in other ways as well. Epic poems were usually about heroic deeds. But lyric poems were about human emotions.

Greek drama was also important during the Golden Age. Many Greek comedies, some written by Aristophanes (ar-ih-STAH-fuh-neez), made fun of common human weakness.

Tragedies in ancient Greece often centered on deep conflicts within families. Some Greek tragedies are still enjoyed by audiences today. Most of these were written by three of ancient Greece's greatest playwrights: Aeschylus (EHS-kuh-luhs), Sophocles (SAH-fuh-kleez), and Euripides (yuh-RIH-puh-deez).

7 Religion

Religion was important to the ancient Greeks. They worshiped many gods and goddesses. Each city-state had at least one special one. They believed that a deity (god or goddess) kept the city-state and its people safe.

The ancient Greeks built beautiful temples for their deities. Each temple had a statue of the god or goddess inside it. People did not attend religious services at these temples. However, worshipers often came to the front of these magnificent buildings with offerings of food or animals.

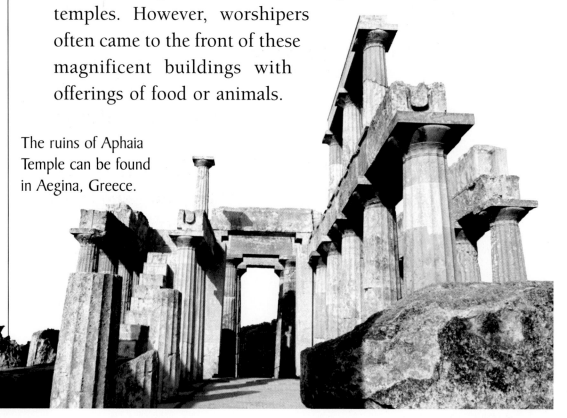

The ruins of Aphaia Temple can be found in Aegina, Greece.

Two Greek horsemen are seen on their way to a religious festival.

There they might ask the god or goddess for help with problems or to tell the future.

The ancient Greeks held religious festivals as well. These celebrations honored the gods and goddesses. People looked forward to the festival entertainment. There were contests in music, athletics, and poetry. Animals were also sacrificed that day to honor the deity.

The ancient Greeks believed their gods and goddesses looked like humans. They thought these deities had human emotions, too. Greek gods and goddesses experienced love, anger, and jealousy. They were also thought to have superhuman strengths and powers.

The ancient Greeks believed that the most

Gods and Goddesses

Aphrodite

Athena

Atlas

Demeter

Gaia

Hades

Hermes

Persephone

Prometheus

Poseidon

Zeus

The ancient Greeks worshipped many gods and goddesses. Each god or goddess oversaw one or more aspects of Greek life.

Aphrodite—Goddess of love and beauty.

Athena—Goddess of warfare, wisdom, and arts and crafts.

Atlas—Part of the special group of gods called the Titans, Greeks believed he held up the sky.

Demeter—Goddess of farming.

Hades—God of the dead and the underworld.

Hermes—Messenger of the gods.

Gaia—Goddess of the Earth.

Persephone—A goddess whom the Greeks used to explain the seasons.

Poseidon—God of the sea.

Prometheus—Part of the special group of gods called the Titans, Greeks believed he gave fire to humans.

Zeus—Ruler of the gods. God of sky and weather.

Zeus was the ruler of the gods. He was known for hurling lightning bolts when angry.

important deities lived on the peak of Mount Olympus. Among these was the chief god, Zeus. Zeus was married to Hera. She was the goddess of marriage. Athena also lived up on Mount Olympus. She was the goddess of wisdom and war. Aphrodite (af-ro-DY-tee) was the goddess of love. The god of the sea was Poseidon (poh-SAI-duhn). There were other Greek gods and goddesses as well. Many stories about these deities are still told today. These are known as Greek myths.

Poseidon ruled the ocean. Although he usually stayed at home, he could sometimes be seen traveling to Olympus over the waves in a chariot drawn by white horses. All sailors looked to him for protection.

Housing

Public buildings in ancient Greece were often beautiful. Temples were even more magnificent. But most people's homes were hardly splendid.

The homes of the poor were small. Often these were just one or two rooms. Rich people's houses tended to be larger. Husbands and wives had separate bedrooms. Sometimes men had another separate room, too. They entertained their male guests there in the evenings.

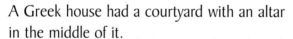

A Greek house had a courtyard with an altar in the middle of it.

Storage jars for oil and grain were found in almost every Greek home.

Many houses in ancient Greece were fairly plain. These houses were made of sun-dried mud bricks. They usually had tiled roofs. The floors were made of tile or stone. These were often built around an open courtyard.

Most homes did not have a lot of furniture. There were usually some beds, chairs, stools, tables, and couches. A stool or chair might be carried from one room to the next when needed.

Indoor plumbing did not exist in ancient Greece. It had not been invented yet. Wooden toilet seats were placed over pots. These were emptied into an outdoor pit. This waste was later collected and taken away from a family's home.

IF I LIVED IN ANCIENT GREECE, I THINK I WOULD REALLY MISS INDOOR PLUMBING.

THAT'S THE GREAT THING ABOUT BEING A DOG. WE DON'T WORRY ABOUT THINGS LIKE THAT.

Food

The ancient Greeks' diet was not very fancy. They used barley and wheat to make porridge and breads. They ate quite a bit of eggs and cheese as well. The ancient Greeks also enjoyed fruits and vegetables. However, oranges, lemons, limes, potatoes, tomatoes, and corn were unknown to them.

Fish was a common dish in ancient Greece. Fish and other foods were cooked in olive oil. The ancient Greeks made this from the olives they grew.

Wine was a popular beverage made from grapes. It was often served with meals. But first it was mixed with water to weaken it.

Only wealthy people in ancient Greece ate meat regularly. They ate beef, pork, goat, sheep, and wild birds. However, chicken was not common. At religious festivals, animals were sacrificed. Then the meat was roasted. Pieces of it were

A fisherman used a tool called a trident to catch fish. A trident is a spear with three prongs.

Olives were used for eating and were pressed into olive oil, which was used for cooking. They are a fruit that grow on trees like the ones in this olive grove in Olympia, Greece.

given out to everyone there. On those occasions, both the rich and poor enjoyed meat.

At times, rich men in ancient Greece invited other males to dinner parties. These were held at their homes. They ate while lying down on dining couches. The food was placed on low tables next to the couches. That way it was easy to reach.

Their wives and children did not go to these gatherings. They ate separately. They sat on chairs and stools when dining.

IT'S NICE TO RELAX AT DINNER.

YEAH, I'M REALLY HUNGRY. TIME TRAVELING TAKES LOTS OF ENERGY.

Clothing

Clothing in ancient Greece was comfortable and flowing. Men as well as women wore chitons. These loose-fitting garments were belted at the waist. They were also fastened at the shoulder with brooches. Chitons are also sometimes called tunics.

The chitons were usually made of linen or wool. Those worn by the poor were made of a rougher material.

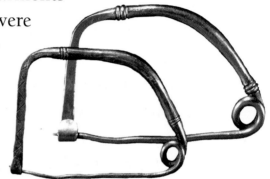

These gold brooches were made around 1050 B.C.

Often the linen and woolen chitons were dyed bright colors. Women in ancient Greece frequently wore red or purple ones.

During the warmer months, the ancient Greeks usually wore sandals. Often the children went barefoot. At home, even the adults went barefoot! Leather boots and shoes were used in the winter. The ancient Greeks also wore cloaks for warmth. These

A Greek woman admires herself in a mirror.
She is wearing a long cloak called a himation.

Leather sandals were worn during the warmer months.

were called himations. They were made from large pieces of rectangular fabric. They were draped or wrapped around the body. Sometimes, Greek men wore shorter cloaks called chlamys. These shorter cloaks kept their arms free so that they could easily swing their swords in battle.

Rich women in ancient Greece wore jewelry. Gold necklaces, bracelets, pins, and earrings were common. They also used makeup. Many powdered their faces to look fairer or paler. They saw this as a sign of beauty. A Greek woman did not want to have a sun tan.

Most women had long hair. They often wore it in buns or ponytails. They used scarves and ribbons as well. Greek men wore hats.

Men exercised regularly to keep strong and fit. They were very proud of their bodies. Male nudity was not a

These gold-plated bracelets are decorated with rams' heads.

Greek men wore chitons into battle. Sometimes, a soldier would be protected with a piece of armor on his chest called a breast plate. The soldiers also wore special leg protectors and carried shields.

This Greek woman is dressed for travel. She is well wrapped up against bad weather in a chiton and himation.

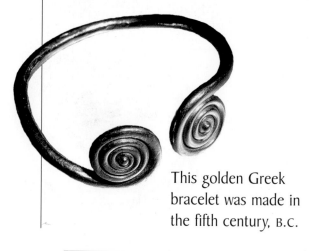

This golden Greek bracelet was made in the fifth century, B.C.

This entranceway to the original Olympic Stadium is in Olympia, Greece. During the 2004 Olympics, the ancient stadium was used for the shot put competition.

cause for shame in ancient Greece. Male athletes competed naked in many events at the Olympics. Women, on the other hand, never left the house unless they were fully dressed. Women also were not allowed to compete or even view the Olympic games.

John Godina of the United States spins around while making a qualifying throw during the Athens 2004 Olympics men's shot put qualification round in Olympia, Greece. The men's and women's shot put was held in the ancient stadium where the original games were played.

Good-bye to Greece

ncient Greece's greatness is unforgettable. Its civilization has influenced our culture in many ways. Today, numerous government buildings are designed like those of ancient Greece. This can be seen in Washington, D.C., as well as in other cities. Ancient Greek dramas are still performed in many countries. College students in the United States and elsewhere take courses in Greek philosophy. Even the Greek alphabet was later developed into the alphabet we use now.

Greek plays were once performed at the Theater of Herod Atticus in Athens. These plays from ancient times are still performed around the world today.

The designer of the United States Supreme Court building was influenced by ancient Greek buildings.

Being in ancient Greece was terrific. But Max and I must be heading home. I have lots to write about, and Max wants to tell his dog pals all about our trip. We are glad you came along with us. Time travel is just more fun with friends. To the time machine!

Farewell Fellow Explorer,

I just wanted to take a moment to tell you a little about the real "Max and me." I am a children's book author, and Max is a small, fluffy, white dog. I almost named him Marshmallow because of how he looked. However, he seems to think he's human—so only a more dignified name would do. Max also seems to think that he is a large, powerful dog. He fearlessly chases after much larger dogs in the neighborhood. Max was thrilled when the artist for this book drew him as a dog several times his size. He felt that someone in the art world had finally captured his true spirit.

In real life, Max is quite a traveler. I have taken him to nearly every state while doing research for different books. We live in Florida, so when we go north I have to pack a sweater for him. When we were in Oregon, it rained and I was glad I brought his raincoat. None of this gear is necessary when time traveling. My "take-off" spot is the computer station, and, as always, Max sits faithfully by my side.

Best Wishes,
Elaine & Max (a small dog with big dreams)

Timeline

2000 B.C.	Small farming villages form in ancient Greece.
1200 B.C.	Mycenae falls.
1200–800 B.C.	The Dark Age in ancient Greece.
490 B.C.	Greeks defeat the invading Persian army at the Battle of Marathon.
480 B.C.	Greeks defeat the Persian forces at the Battle of Salamis.
457 B.C.	Male commoners are allowed to hold any public office in Athens.
432 B.C.	The Parthenon is completed.
431 B.C.	The start of the Peloponnesian War.
400s–300s B.C.	The Golden Age in ancient Greece.
338 B.C.	King Philip II of Macedonia defeats the Greek city-states at the Battle of Chaeronea.

334 B.C.	Alexander the Great invades Persia with a combined Greek and Macedonian army.
200s B.C.	Rome becomes a great power.
140s B.C.	Rome takes over both Macedonia and Greece.

Glossary

agora—A marketplace in ancient Greece.

astronomer—A scientist who studies the stars, planets, and other bodies in space.

circumference—The distance around something.

comedy—A funny play, motion picture, or television show.

drama—A story that is written for actors to perform on the stage.

literature—Written works, such as plays, poem, and novels.

lyre—a musical instrument with strings that is like a harp.

offering—A gift left for a god or goddess.

peninsula—A narrow strip of land extending out to the sea that is almost completely surrounded by water.

philosophy—The study of wisdom and truth.

rival—Someone you are competing against.

tragedy—A serious play with a sad ending.

truce—An agreement to stop fighting.

For More Information

Ashworth, Leon. *Gods and Goddesses of Ancient Greece.* Mankato, Minn.: Smart Apple Media, 2003.

Connolly, Peter. *Ancient Greece.* New York: Oxford University Press, 2001.

Fanelli, Sara. *Mythological Monsters of Ancient Greece.* Boston: Candlewick, 2002.

Macdonald, Fiona. *You Wouldn't Want to Be a Slave in Ancient Greece!* Danbury, Conn.: Franklin Watts, 2000.

Pearson, Anne. *Eyewitness: Ancient Greece.* New York: DK Publishing, 2000.

Wroble, Lisa A. *Kids in Ancient Greece.* New York: Powerkids Press, 2001.

Internet Addresses

History For Kids

This Web site offers good information on the food, clothing, and art of ancient Greece. Don't miss the fun section on projects on Greece.

<http://www.historyforkids.org>

BBC History: Ancient Greece

Be sure to see the "For Kids" section of this Web site for information on the Olympic games, ancient Greek theater, and much more.

<http://www.bbc.co.uk/history/ancient/greeks>

Under the "History" heading at the left, click on "Ancient History." Then, click on "Greeks."

Mythweb

Go to this Web site to learn all about heroes, gods, and monsters found in Greek myths.

<http://www.mythweb.com>

Index